KB276131

O. Henry's Short Stories

Happy House

About Wise & Wide

- A systematic 6-level English reading program based on Lexile® measures
- Diverse and interesting topics chosen from the elementary curriculums of Korea and English speaking western countries
- Well-written books in various forms including fiction stories, descriptive texts, and classics retold
- The informative but original fiction stories grab your interest, leading to the easy and clear understanding of the educational content.
- Improve thinking skills with solid after-reading activities at all levels of the series.

Wise & Wide is a 6-level English reading program that consists of 60 books and each level is systematically divided by Lexile® measures. The Lexile® Framework for Reading is the most popular reading measuring system in American formal education curriculums and many English programs. Over 20 out of 50 states in the U.S. mark Lexile® measures directly on students' final report cards and over 300 well-known publishers adopt and use Lexile® measures.

Experience many kinds of readings written by professional writers from the U.S. and England. They used interesting topics that were carefully chosen after analyzing elementary curriculums from around the world including Korea, the U.S., England, and Australia among many others. Comprehensive after-reading activities including graphic organizers, speaking tasks, and After-reading Tests are ready for you.

Levels in the series and their corresponding Lexile® measures

Level	Lexile® measures	U.S. Grade
Level 1	Below 200L	Pre K - K
Level 2	190L - 400L	Lower Grade 1
Level 3	350L - 530L	Upper Grade 1
Level 4	420L - 650L	Grade 2
Level 5	520L - 940L	Grade 3 - 4
Level 6	830L - 1070L	Grade 5 - 6

* Smart Readers: Wise & Wide level 1 is applicable to the preschool level in the U.S.

* The source of the relationship between Lexile® measures and U.S. school grades: CCSS(Common Core State Standards) FOR ENGLISH LANGUAGE ARTS, APPENDIX A (2012, which is used by 45 states in the U.S.)

Topic List

	Level 1	Level 2	Level 3	Level 4	Level 5	Level 6
Book 1	Science>Biology: The hibernation of animals Story	Science>Biology: Living and nonliving things Story	Science>Biology> Animals & the Environment: Sea otters Story	Environment> Living with nature: The diver & the persimmon tree Story	Science>Biology> Animal: Amazing animals of the Amazon Story	Science>Biology: Germs, transmitted diseases Story
Book 2	Literature> World classics: Aesop's fables Story	Literature> Traditional fairy tale: Old tales about stones Story	Social Studies> Economy: To run a business to make and save money Story	Science>Biology> Plants: Photosynthesis Story	Science>Earth science: Earth's layers,earthquakes, volcanoes, and earth's atmosphere Report	Mathematics> Sequence: The golden ratio & the Fibonacci sequence Story
Book 3	Science>Physics: How shadows are formed Story	Literature> World classics: Peter Pan Story	Science>Scientific technology: Nanobots Story	Literature>Myths: World's creation stories Story	Literature> Legend: The story of King Arthur Story	Literature>Myths: Constellation myths Story
Book 4	Literature> Traditional literature: The Talmud Story	Science>Biology> Animal: Polar bears Story	Science>Biology> Animal: Mountain gorillas Story	Social Studies> Cultural anthropology: Amazing ancient cultures of the world Story	Science> Earth science: Clouds and weather Story	Literature> Human & animals: The friendship between a girl and a horse Story
Book 5	Social Studies> Ethics: Rules in daily life Story	Science>Biology: The five senses Report	Social Studies> Cultural anthropology: Astonishing festivals Report	Art>Music: Stories from two operas Story	Social Studies> World culture & history: The Renaissance Story	Sports> Board sports: Surfing & snowboarding Story
Book 6	Social Studies> World geography & travel: Tourist attractions around the world Story	Science>Biology> Animal: Dinosaurs Story	Science> Astronomy: The solar system Story	Social Studies> People: Three great people who overcome hardships Story	Science>Scientific technology: The wonderful world of robots Report	Art>Music: Composers of the Romantic Era Report
Book 7	Science> Space science: The life of astronauts Report	Social Studies> Cultural anthropology: Mythological monsters from around the world Report	Mathematics> Elementary mathematics: Numbers, measurement, shapes and data Report	Science & Social Studies> Technology & culture: Inventions from around the world Report	Art>Works of art: Famous paintings Report	Social Studies> Human & animals: Animals in action for human Report
Book 8	Social Studies> Cultural anthropology: Various living cultures of the world Story	Art>Music: Instruments in the orchestra Story	Social Studies> Life safety: Learning and using outdoor survival skills Story	Social Studies> History: The California Gold Rush Report	Social Studies & Science> Psychology: Psychology in everyday life Story	Literature> World classics: The Merchant of Venice Story
Book 9	Social Studies> Jobs: Interviews about jobs Report	Science>Scientific technology: Developments in technology in different times Story	Social Studies> Politics>Election: Running for 3rd grade class president Story	Literature> World classics: Stories of Sherlock Holmes Story	Literature> World classics: Adrift in the Pacific Story	Social Studies> History & People: Great world leaders in history Report
Book 10	Literature>Traditional fairy tale: Eastern and Western folk tales on the same theme Story	Sports>Winter sports: Various aspects of some Winter Olympic sports Report	Literature> World classics: Short stories by O. Henry Story	Sports> Ball games: Various aspects of popular ball games Report	Social Studies> History: Famous events that changed world history Report	Art & Social Studies> Art: Stories about the creation, distribution, and preservation of paintings Report

* 10 books in each level will be published.

How to Use This Book

●Before Reading

You can easily find the topic and what kind of story you are about to read.

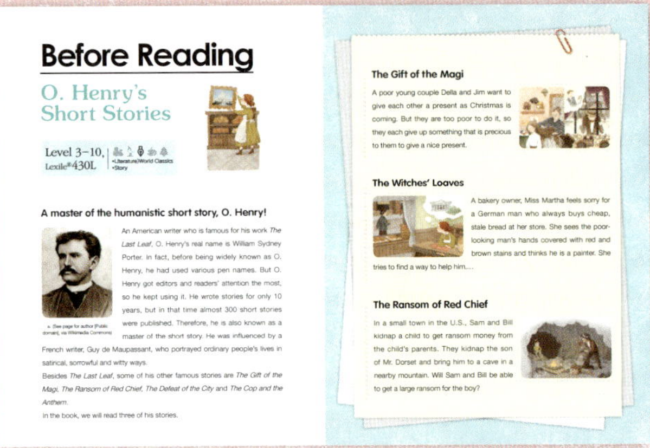

●The text

All the stories were written by professional writers from the U.S. and England, so you will read authentic and appropriate English sentences and expressions in every book in the series.

●Pop Quiz

Check out right away if you understand what you have just read by solving a pop quiz that checks your comprehension.

●Key Words

The key words and expressions on each page are listed for you to easily study them.

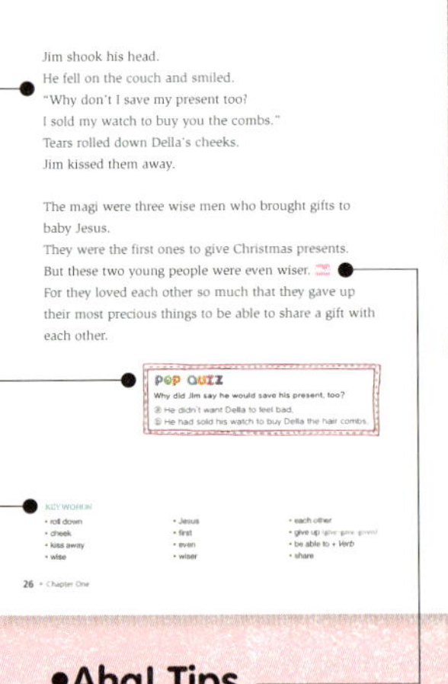

●Aha! Tips

Download free Korean explanations at *www.ihappyhouse.co.kr* for all of the sentences marked with "Aha!". These explain cultural, scientific, and economic knowledge or they deal with aspects of English such as grammatical structures or idiomatic expressions. There are lots of "Aha! Tips" to help you understand the text.

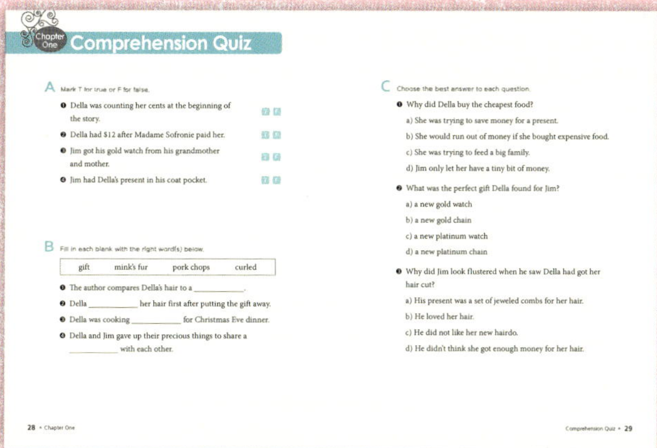

•Comprehension Quiz

After reading one chapter, solve various questions to find out if you fully understand the content.

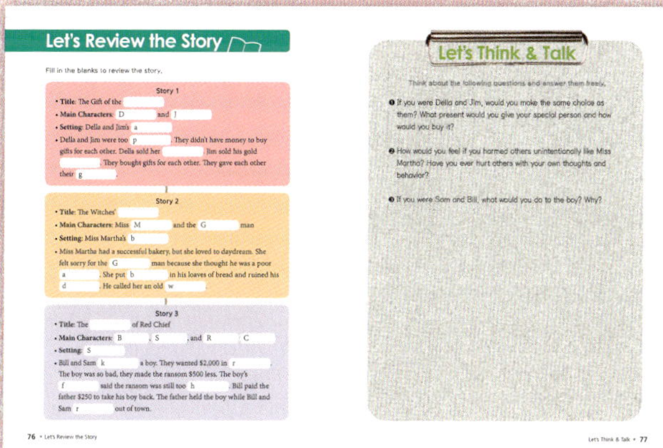

•Let's Review the Story / •Let's Think & Talk

Fill in the blanks in the organizer to summarize the whole story. Express your own thinking and feelings about the story by answering the questions. You can build up logic and reasoning skills for your essay examinations in the future.

Appendix

Audio CD

In the CD audio book form, the texts are read vividly by American professional voice actors. (MP3 files downloaded for free)

After-reading Test

Solve an additionally provided After-reading Test for each book.

The Korean translation, Answer Keys, a Word Quiz, a Word List, and Aha! Tips for each book

You can download them for free at *www.ihappyhouse.co.kr* or *www.darakwon.co.kr*

Before Reading

O. Henry's Short Stories

Level 3-10, Lexile® 430L | •Literature〉World Classics •Story

A master of the humanistic short story, O. Henry!

▲ (See page for author [Public domain], via Wikimedia Commons)

An American writer who is famous for his work *The Last Leaf*, O. Henry's real name is William Sydney Porter. In fact, before being widely known as O. Henry, he had used various pen names. But O. Henry got editors and readers' attention the most, so he kept using it. He wrote stories for only 10 years, but in that time almost 300 short stories were published. Therefore, he is also known as a master of the short story. He was influenced by a French writer, Guy de Maupassant, who portrayed ordinary people's lives in satirical, sorrowful and witty ways.

Besides *The Last Leaf*, some of his other famous stories are *The Gift of the Magi, The Ransom of Red Chief, The Defeat of the City* and *The Cop and the Anthem*.

In the book, we will read three of his stories.

The Gift of the Magi

A poor young couple Della and Jim want to give each other a present as Christmas is coming. But they are too poor to do it, so they each give up something that is precious to them to give a nice present.

The Witches' Loaves

A bakery owner, Miss Martha feels sorry for a German man who always buys cheap, stale bread at her store. She sees the poor-looking man's hands covered with red and brown stains and thinks he is a painter. She tries to find a way to help him....

The Ransom of Red Chief

In a small town in the U.S., Sam and Bill kidnap a child to get ransom money from the child's parents. They kidnap the son of Mr. Dorset and bring him to a cave in a nearby mountain. Will Sam and Bill be able to get a large ransom for the boy?

Contents

O. Henry's Short Stories

O. Henry's Short Stories

Chapter One

The Gift of the Magi

A beautiful young woman sat in her apartment on a cold winter day counting her money.

Della loved her husband Jim more than anything.

Tomorrow would be Christmas.

He deserved the best present she could give him.

The last cent fell into her lap.

"Oh, no!" Della shook her head.

"I only have one dollar and eighty-seven cents.

What can I buy with that?"

She fell back on the worn-out couch and cried.

"I've been buying the cheapest food and saving every cent.

Still, this is all I have."

She looked around the old, cold apartment.

Things were broken.

The mailbox was broken.

The doorbell was broken.

They had no money to fix them.

The apartment rent cost them $8 a week.

This may not sound like much.

But Jim only made $20 a week.

After the rent and expenses, there was never any money left over.

- **look around** (*cf.* around)
- **thing**
- **be broken** (*cf.* break (break-broke-broken))
- **mailbox**
- **doorbell**
- **fix**
- **rent**
- **cost** (cost-cost(ed)-cost(ed))
- **week**
- **may +** *Verb*
- **sound like**
- **make** (make-made-made)
- **expense**
- **never**
- **any**
- **leave over** (leave-left-left)
- **gray**
- **walk along**
- **fence**
- **backyard**
- **grand**
- **just any**
- **do** (do-did-done)

Della looked out the window at the gray winter day.
She watched a gray cat walk along the gray fence in her gray backyard.
She wanted to buy Jim something special. **Aha!**
He deserved something grand.
Just any old gift would never do.

Della looked in the mirror.

Her eyes lit up with excitement.

She had an idea!

She had the most beautiful hair of any woman. **Aha!**

Her hair was her crowning glory.

It was her most precious possession.

She shook out her thick brown hair.

It hung down past her knees!

It shone in the light from the windows.

A mink's fur couldn't be softer or shinier than her hair.

KEY WORDS

- look in the mirror
- eye
- light up with (light-lit-lit)
- excitement
- have an idea (have-had-had)
- crowning glory
- precious
- possession
- shake out

- thick
- hang down (hang-hung-hung)
- past
- shine (shine-shone-shone)
- mink
- fur
- softer
- shinier

"There are always people who want to buy hair, especially hair like mine," she told the mirror.

Before she could change her mind, she pinned her hair up, threw on her old brown coat, and placed a ratty brown hat on her head.

Looking down, she saw a single tear drop onto the worn carpet.

KEY WORDS

- always
- especially
- mine
- pin up
- **throw on** (throw-threw-thrown)

- place
- ratty
- tear drop
- carpet

She walked until she saw the sign for a salon.

It read, Madame Sofronie: Hair Goods of All Kinds.

"Will you buy my hair?"

Della asked the old woman in the store.

"It depends." The woman sniffed.

"Take off your hat and let me see it."

Della took off her hat.

"Hmm."

The old woman smiled and ran her hand over Della's

long, thick and shiny hair.

She picked up a handful of the heavy brown locks.

"Twenty dollars," was all she said.

Twenty dollars!

That was a whole week's wages for Jim!

"Do it," Della said. "Cut it quickly and pay me."

KEY WORDS

▪ until	▪ store	▪ pick up
▪ sign	▪ depend	▪ handful
▪ salon	▪ sniff	▪ heavy
▪ **read** (read-read-read)	▪ **take off** (take-took-taken)	▪ lock
▪ madame	▪ **let** + *Object* + *Verb*	▪ whole
▪ goods	▪ **run** (run-ran-run)	▪ wage(s)
▪ kind	▪ hand	▪ pay

LOTION

Camellia

As soon as Della was relieved of her heavy burden, she
ran down the street to the local stores.

She peered in the windows.

She looked at the display shelves.

Finally, after two hours, she found it.

The perfect gift.

It was an elegant platinum watch chain.

It was the only one of its kind in all the stores around.

It would look perfect on Jim's gold watch.

He was so proud of that watch.

It had been passed down from father to son since Jim's
grandfather had been alive.

Jim carried it on an old, battered leather band.

The gold watch was Jim's most prized possession.

KEY WORDS

- as soon as
- relieve
- burden
- local
- peer in
- display
- shelves
- finally

- find (find-found-found)
- perfect
- elegant
- platinum
- chain
- be proud of (cf. proud)
- so
- pass down

- from A to B
- since
- alive
- carry
- battered
- leather
- band
- prized

Yes, Della knew she had to have the chain.

She paid $21 for it.

Then she ran home with her eighty-seven cents in change.

As soon as Della got back to the apartment, she put the gift away and began fixing her hair.

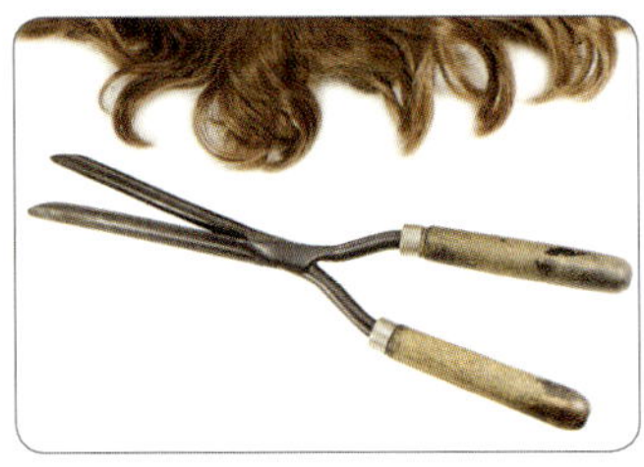

▲ an old-style curling iron

She curled it with her curling iron. She ran her fingers through it, setting the curls just right.

"I hope Jim doesn't kill me when he sees my new hairdo," she said to herself.

She put on a pot of coffee, and heated up the stove.

They were having a pork chop dinner for Christmas Eve.

Della heard Jim's footstep on the stairs outside the apartment.

She said a little prayer.

"Please Lord, let Jim still think I'm pretty."

Jim walked in, looking tired and cold.

He took off his old coat.

He blew on his cold hands and rubbed them together.

Della smiled at him. "Welcome home!"

Jim stared at Della.

He stared at her hair.

Della ran her shaking fingers over her hair.

"Don't worry, Jim.

My hair will grow back.

I cut it so I could buy you a nice Christmas present."

Jim's mouth hung open.

"You cut off your hair?"

"Yes." Della took his hands in hers.

Jim looked around the tiny apartment.

"It's gone?"

"Yes." Della kissed his fingers.

"I sold it. I love you so much that I would do anything

for you." `Aha!`

Jim hugged her.

"I love you just the way you are.

I love you with hair or without hair."

He looked into her eyes.

"I brought you a present."

He reached into his coat pocket and pulled out a small package.

KEY WORDS

- hug
- without
- **bring** (bring-brought-brought)
- reach into
- pull out
- package

Della tore open her gift.

It was a set of combs to hold up her hair.

They sparkled with jewels on them.

The combs had caught her eye in a department store window.

She never thought she would own them.

They were too expensive.

KEY WORDS

- **tear open** (tear-tore-torn)
- **a set of**
- **comb**
- **hold up** (hold-held-held)
- **sparkle**
- **jewel**
- **catch one's eye(s)** (catch-caught-caught)
- **department store**
- **own**
- **too**
- **expensive**

Della touched her hair again and smiled.

"I'll keep them safe until my hair grows long again.

It grows so fast!"

She handed Jim a package.

"Here is my present for you!"

Della watched with excitement as Jim opened his

present.

He lifted the platinum chain.

"I looked all over for this!" Della told him.

"It's going to look
so good with your
watch.
Go ahead, get out
your watch.
I want to see it with
the chain."

- touch
- keep (keep-kept-kept)
- safe
- Here is[are] ~.
- as

- lift
- look all over (*cf.* all over)
- be going to + *Verb*
- go ahead (go-went-gone)
- get out

Jim shook his head.

He fell on the couch and smiled.

"Why don't I save my present too?

I sold my watch to buy you the combs."

Tears rolled down Della's cheeks.

Jim kissed them away.

The magi were three wise men who brought gifts to baby Jesus.

They were the first ones to give Christmas presents.

But these two young people were even wiser. 

For they loved each other so much that they gave up their most precious things to be able to share a gift with each other.

POP QUIZ

Why did Jim say he would save his present, too?

ⓐ He didn't want Della to feel bad.
ⓑ He had sold his watch to buy Della the hair combs.

KEY WORDS

- roll down
- cheek
- kiss away
- wise

- Jesus
- first
- even
- wiser

- each other
- give up (give-gave-given)
- be able to + *Verb*
- share

Comprehension Quiz

A Mark T for true or F for false.

❶ Della was counting her cents at the beginning of the story.　　T　F

❷ Della had $12 after Madame Sofronie paid her.　　T　F

❸ Jim got his gold watch from his grandmother and mother.　　T　F

❹ Jim had Della's present in his coat pocket.　　T　F

B Fill in each blank with the right word(s) below.

gift	mink's fur	pork chops	curled

❶ The author compares Della's hair to a ______________.

❷ Della ______________ her hair first after putting the gift away.

❸ Della was cooking ______________ for Christmas Eve dinner.

❹ Della and Jim gave up their precious things to share a ______________ with each other.

❶ Why did Della buy the cheapest food?

  a) She was trying to save money for a present.

  b) She would run out of money if she bought expensive food.

  c) She was trying to feed a big family.

  d) Jim only let her have a tiny bit of money.

❷ What was the perfect gift Della found for Jim?

  a) a new gold watch

  b) a new gold chain

  c) a new platinum watch

  d) a new platinum chain

❸ Why did Jim look flustered when he saw Della had got her hair cut?

  a) His present was a set of jeweled combs for her hair.

  b) He loved her hair.

  c) He did not like her new hairdo.

  d) He didn't think she got enough money for her hair.

Chapter Two

The Witches' Loaves

Miss Martha Meacham was arranging bread on the shelf of her bakery window.

She was proud of her little business.

She loved the three steps up to her bakery.

She loved the sound of the bell tinkling whenever someone opened the door.

She was proud that she had saved $2,000 in her bank account.

She smiled happily, showing her two false teeth. 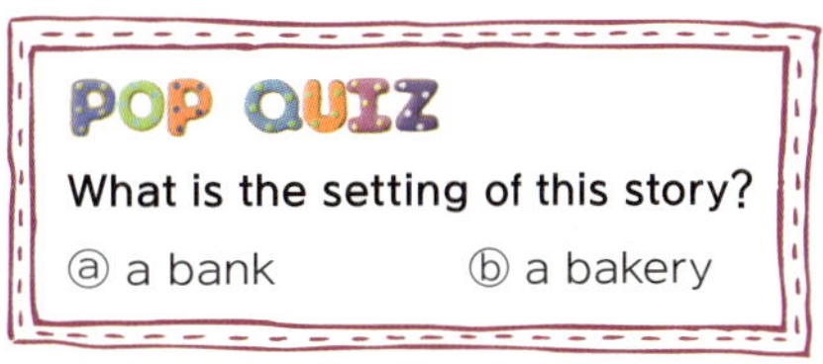

She was forty years old, and in her mind, she was very successful.

POP QUIZ

What is the setting of this story?

ⓐ a bank   ⓑ a bakery

KEY WORDS

- witch
- loaves
- arrange
- bakery
- business

- step
- up to
- tinkling
- whenever
- bank account

- happily
- show
- false tooth (*cf.* teeth)
- successful

In walked a customer, a middle-aged man. **Aha!**

He placed his order in a German accent.

He wore a neatly trimmed, pointy brown beard.

It contrasted with his old clothes.

They were mended and wrinkled.

Miss Martha's sold soft and delicious fresh bread for 5 cents a loaf.

Stale bread sold for 5 cents for two loaves.

Every time this man came in, he bought stale bread.

Miss Martha thought, "Poor man. He must not be able to afford fresh bread."

He handed Miss Martha the coin for his bread.

As he did, Miss Martha noticed something odd.

His fingers were stained red and brown.

"Perhaps he is an artist," she imagined.

KEY WORDS

- customer
- middle-aged
- place an order
- German
- accent
- **wear** (wear-wore-worn)
- neatly
- trim
- pointy
- beard
- contrast with
- clothes
- mend
- wrinkle
- delicious
- fresh
- stale
- poor
- must + *Verb*
- afford
- notice
- odd
- stain
- perhaps
- imagine

She daydreamed.

"He probably lives in an artist's loft.

He probably paints all day until sundown.

It is so sad that he is too poor to buy my delicious breads and rolls. Aha!

But that is the way life goes for an artist."

You see, Miss Martha had a sympathetic heart.

She wished she could feed the German something better.

KEY WORDS

- daydream
- probably
- loft
- all day

- sundown
- roll
- go for
- sympathetic

- heart
- wish
- feed (feed-fed-fed)
- better

The next morning, she propped a painting of Venice behind her bakery counter. The painting had a beautiful white marble palace. Gondolas, the romantic boats used in Venice, floated on the water in front of it. Miss Martha hoped the German would notice the painting.

KEY WORDS

- prop
- Venice
- behind
- counter
- marble
- palace
- gondola
- romantic
- boat
- use
- float
- in front of (*cf.* front)
- hope

The bell on the door tinkled.

The sound was a delight, but even better was the sight

of the German.

He looked at the painting.

"I do love art," Miss Martha said. Aha!

She wrapped his bread.

"It is not so good," the German said.

"No? Why do you say that?" she asked.

"The perspective is not true.

The picture does not look real."

He paid for his bread and left.

POP QUIZ

What did the German say about the painting?
ⓐ The picture does not look real.
ⓑ It is quite beautiful.

- tinkle
- delight
- sight
- wrap

- perspective
- genius
- yet
- what if ~?

- support
- after all
- last
- while

"He must be a genius," Miss Martha thought.

"Yet he is also kind."

She daydreamed again.

What if she could help the German?

What if she could feed him, and support him?

After all, she had $2,000 in the bank.

That could last a while in helping a poor artist.

The next day, he bought stale bread again.

Miss Martha thought he looked thin.

She wished she could give him a cake or a pie or a

sweet roll.

However, there was no way to give it to him without

being rude.

▲ quince

That night, Miss Martha made a
special face cream.
She mashed quince seeds and
mixed them with borax.
It might lighten her skin.

Then she took her blue dotted silk dress out of the

closet.

Surely he would notice her wearing this pretty dress.

KEY WORDS

- thin
- pie
- however
- rude
- face cream
- mash
- quince

- seed
- mix
- borax
- lighten
- dotted
- silk
- out of

- closet
- surely
- fire truck
- drive (drive·drove·driven)
- horn
- blare
- flash

The German came the next day.

Just when Miss Martha was getting his stale bread, a fire truck drove past.

Its horns blared.

Its lights flashed.

The man ran to the front window to watch it.

"Aha! This is my chance," Miss Martha thought.

While he looked out the window, she grabbed a knife.
She cut the loaves in half.
She spread a thick layer of butter on the bread.

Next, she put the loaves back together, hiding the butter inside.

When the German came back to the counter, Miss Martha was already wrapping up the loaves.

She smiled at him.

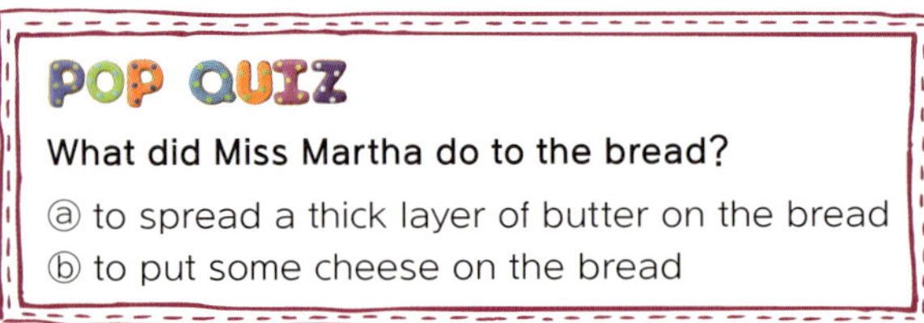

POP QUIZ

What did Miss Martha do to the bread?

ⓐ to spread a thick layer of butter on the bread
ⓑ to put some cheese on the bread

KEY WORDS

- chance
- grab
- in half

- spread (spread-spread-spread)
- layer
- put back

- hide (hide-hid-hidden)
- inside
- already

Would he be surprised?

Would he be happy?

As she watched him leave the bakery, she daydreamed again. **Aha!**

She imagined him taking the bread back to his loft.

She imagined him taking a bite out of the bread.

She saw the delight on his face as he tasted the sweet creamy butter.

Oh, he would be happy for sure!

- surprised
- **take a bite** (*cf.* bite (bite-bit-bitten))
- taste
- creamy
- for sure

Stupid
fool!!

Later that day, two men stomped up the three stairs.

The bell on the door sounded angry.

The German stormed into the bakery.

A young man followed him.

The German's face grew red as he yelled.

"Stupid fool!"

He shook his fists at Miss Martha.

She backed away from the counter.

He banged his hands on the countertop.

"You old witch! You ruined me!

You spoiled everything!"

The young man dragged the German outside and talked
to him.

KEY WORDS

- later
- stomp
- storm into
- follow
- yell

- stupid
- fool
- fist
- back away from
- bang

- countertop
- ruin
- spoil
- drag

The young man came back in alone.

"What happened?

What does that man mean, I spoiled everything?"

Miss Martha's lips trembled.

"That man's name is Blumberger," the young man said.

"He draws plans for architects.

He is a draftsman."

"Yes, but why is he angry?"

The man leaned against the counter.

"You see, he entered a contest.

It is for a drawing of a new city hall."

Miss Martha thought Blumberger must be talented to enter such a contest.

KEY WORDS

- alone
- happen
- mean (mean-meant-meant)
- tremble
- draw (draw-drew-drawn)

- plan
- architect
- draftsman
- lean (against)
- you see

- enter a contest (*cf.* enter)
- drawing
- city hall
- talented
- such

The man continued talking.

"Blumberger worked on his drawing for three months."

"That's a long time," Miss Martha said.

"Yes, it is. Here is how he works. **Aha!**

First, he draws with a pencil.

After he finishes a section, he traces it with ink."

"It sounds like a lot of work," Miss Martha said.

"Yes, it is," the young man agreed.

"After he traces a part in ink, then he erases all of the pencil marks.

Do you know the best way to erase pencil marks?"

"With an eraser?" Miss Martha asked.

"No." The young man shook his head.

"There is a way that is even better than using any eraser."

The man tapped a finger on a loaf of stale bread.

"This works better than any rubber eraser.

Stale bread erases the pencil marks.

He rubs it on the paper.

Then he brushes the crumbs away."

Miss Martha's eyes widened.

"But when he used the bread today, the butter you put

on it smeared all over the drawing.

The ink smeared. The drawing is ruined."

Miss Martha let out a sad breath of air now.

She went back to her bedroom.

She took off her pretty silk dress.

She put on her old one.

She threw the special face cream into the trashcan.

Then she went back to work.

KEY WORDS

- tap
- rubber
- brush away
- crumb
- widen
- smear
- let out
- breath
- trashcan

Comprehension Quiz

A Mark T for true or F for false.

❶ The German bought loaves of stale bread every time he came into the bakery.　T　F

❷ A fire truck drove past the front window when the German came in one day.　T　F

❸ Miss Martha put honey and almonds into her face cream.　T　F

❹ The contest the German had entered was for a drawing of a new city hall.　T　F

B What did Miss Martha do when the German was looking out the window? Put the sentences in order.

❶ She put butter inside the loaves of bread.

❷ She wrapped up the bread loaves.

❸ She cut the loaves in half.

❹ She put the loaves back together.

________ → ________ → ________ → ________

 Choose the best answer to each question.

❶ What did Miss Martha think was odd about the German?

a) His beard was braided.

b) His hair was messy.

c) His clothes were always neatly pressed.

d) His fingers were stained red and brown.

❷ What did Miss Martha daydream about doing with her $2,000?

a) selling her bakery and buying a bigger one

b) supporting the German so he could do his artwork

c) buying another painting

d) buying a wedding ring

❸ Why did Miss Martha's eyes grow wide while the young man was talking?

a) She wanted to see the German clearly.

b) She saw a fire truck go by on the street.

c) She realized the butter in her bread ruined the drawing.

d) The room was dark and she couldn't see.

Chapter Three

The Ransom of Red Chief

Some people think me and my friend Bill are bad guys.

But wait until I tell you my story.

Then see what you think.

Once me and Bill needed $2,000 cash fast.

We went to a town called Summit.

Don't let the name fool you.

This town was as flat as a cast iron griddle. **Aha!**

It was a small town, with a small police force.

▲ griddle

The people who lived there had lots of kids and they were proud of them.

It was the perfect place for a kidnapping.

KEY WORDS

- ransom
- chief
- guy
- wait
- once
- need

- cash
- called
- summit
- flat
- cast iron
- griddle

- police force
- lots of
- kid
- kidnapping (*cf*. kidnap)

Ebenezer Dorset lived in Summit.

He was a strict man, always followed the rules.

He went to church every Sunday.

He approved home loans for the local bank.

Mr. Dorset had one ten-year-old son.

We figured the boy must be special to his dad.

We decided this was the boy to kidnap.

About two miles away from Summit we found a cave in a mountain.

We bought supplies and stored them in the cave.

Outside the town in a small village we rented a horse and buggy.

Just after sundown, we drove to the Dorset house.

The kid was outside throwing rocks at a poor little kitten.

Bill smiled at the boy.

"Hey, kid! Do you want some candy?"

The kid stared at him a minute.

Then he threw a piece of a brick at Bill.

It caught him right in the eye.

"Ouch! That hurt!"

Bill rubbed his eye.

He leaned toward me and said, "That's going to cost his father an extra $500." Aha!

We jumped out of the buggy and grabbed the boy.

He fought.

He howled like a cat.

But we finally got him in the buggy and drove him to the cave.

I went back to the village to return the horse and buggy.

Then I walked back to the cave.

When I got back, I couldn't believe what I saw.

The boy had two turkey feathers in his hair.

He stood by the fire shouting, "I am Red Chief!"

He stopped me with his hand.

"I dare you to enter!"

Bill nodded.

"We've been playing Indian.

Red Chief says he's going to scalp me."

I eyed the bruises on Bill's face and legs.

"That kid can kick," Bill told me.

The boy stomped over and poked a stick at me.

"You are Snake Eye the Spy!

I'm going to burn you at the stake!"

"It looks like you're having fun," I told the kid.

He whooped and danced until Bill served us dinner.

All through dinner, the boy didn't stop talking.

Finally, Bill was worn out.

"Hey, kid, do you want to go home?" he asked.

"Nope. Home is no fun.

I hate going to school."

"It's late," I told the boy.

"We have to go to bed."

It was 11 p.m.

But the boy stayed up for three more hours playing

Indian.

KEY WORDS

- bruise
- kick
- poke
- stick
- spy
- burn at the stake (*cf.* burn/stake)
- have fun (*cf.* fun)
- whoop

- serve
- all through
- be worn out
- hate
- go to bed
- p.m.
- stay up

I had terrible dreams.

I dreamed I was chained to a tree by a pirate.

I woke up when Bill screamed in fear.

Red Chief was sitting on Bill's chest with a knife in his hand.

"I'm going to scalp you!"

He grabbed Bill's hair.

Bill didn't sleep anymore that night.

Neither did I. Aha!

I remembered that Red Chief was planning to burn me at the stake.

Bill asked, "Do you think anyone will pay to get this brat back?"

I nodded. "Sure they will. Parents love kids like that."

KEY WORDS

- **have a dream** (*cf.* dream)
- **terrible**
- **be chained to**
- **pirate**
- **wake up** (wake-woke-woken)
- **scream**
- **in fear** (*cf.* fear)
- **chest**
- **anymore**
- **neither**
- **brat**

As soon as it was morning light, I went to the
mountaintop.
I looked down on the town.
I wanted to see if people were acting worried.
Maybe they were setting up search parties to find the
boy.

But wait until I tell you what I saw.

No one was looking for the boy.

A farmer was plowing his fields.

No one was hanging up missing person signs.

Peace and quiet reigned in Summit.

- mountaintop
- if
- act
- worried
- maybe
- set up

- search party
- look for
- farmer
- plow
- field
- hang up

- missing
- person
- peace and quiet
- reign

I went back to the cave.

The boy had a big

rock in his hand.

It was the size of an

egg.

He had Bill trapped

in a corner.

"Sam!"

Bill called to me.

"This kid took a hot potato off the fire and smashed it

on my back!

It hurt so bad that I hit him on the ears."

He rubbed his back.

"Do you have a gun?"

Red Chief whooped.

The rock went flying and hit Bill behind the ear.

Bill fell onto the hot water pan on the fire.

I raced over and pulled him off.

I poured cold water over his head and back.

"You better behave!"

I yelled at the kid.

"If you don't, I'll take you home!"

"I was just having fun," the boy said.

"I didn't mean to hurt him."

"You need to apologize to Bill."

The boy sat down on a rock to think.

I walked over to where Bill was sitting.

"Bill, I have to go to Poplar Cove, a nearby village."

Bill shook his head.

"No, Sam, no!

Don't leave me here for long with Red Chief."

"I won't be long," I promised.

"I just have to mail the ransom note."

"I think you should lower the ransom by $500.

That boy is a wildcat!"

The note told Dorset to leave his answer in a box on a fence outside of Summit at 8:30 p.m.

We signed it, "Two Desperate Men."

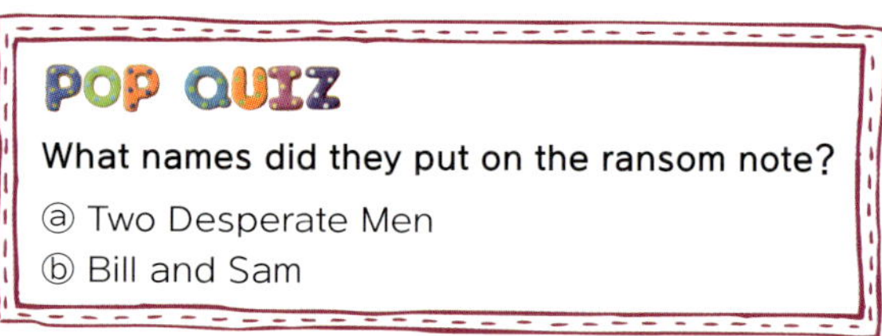

KEY WORDS

- walk over to
- cove
- nearby
- won't
- promise

- mail
- note
- should + *Verb*
- lower
- wildcat

- desperate
- about that time
- another
- right then

About that time, the boy decided he wanted to play
another game.

"You be the horse!" he told Bill.

He jumped on his back.

Bill's eyes looked like the eyes of a rabbit caught in a
trap.

Right then, I wished the ransom was only $1,000.

I left to mail the note.

When I got back to the cave, Bill and the boy were gone.

"Bill!" I called.

Bill came out from hiding.

"Sam, I've been tortured," he told me.

"He rode me like a horse for 90 miles.

Then he gave me sand to eat!

He never stopped talking!

He kicked me and bit me."

He shook his head.

"I'm so tired. I sent the boy home."

I looked over Bill's shoulder.

The boy was sneaking up behind him.

"Say, Bill?" I asked.

"Do you have a weak heart?"

"No," said Bill.

"That's good," I told him.

"I want you to turn around and look."

KEY WORDS

- be tortured
- ride (ride-rode-ridden)
- sand
- send (send-sent-sent)
- shoulder
- sneak up
- weak
- turn around

Bill turned around.

When he saw the boy, he almost fainted.

His skin went chalk white.

I tried to reassure Bill.

"We'll be done with the job by midnight. I promise."

I went to get the answer to the ransom note, brought it back to the cave and read it.

"Dear Two Desperate Men,

Your ransom is too high.

How about you bring the boy home?

If you pay me $250, I'll take him back."

POP QUIZ

Why did Bill almost faint when he saw the boy behind him?

ⓐ The boy said, "Boo!" and scared Bill.
ⓑ He thought the boy had gone home.

KEY WORDS

- almost
- faint
- chalk
- try to + *Verb*
- reassure
- be done with

- midnight
- dear
- how about ~?
- take + *Person* + back
- ain't
- nothing

- pass up
- get rid of
- daddy
- silver
- rifle
- hunting

I showed the letter to Bill.

He smiled.

"Sam, that's great! $250 ain't nothing!

You won't pass up this chance to get rid of him, will you?"

I told the boy, "Hey, kid. Your daddy bought you a silver rifle.

He says you're going bear hunting.

We have to take you home."

At midnight, we knocked on Dorset's door.

"No!" The boy howled.

He grabbed Bill's leg and wouldn't let go.

Dorset peeled the boy off Bill's leg like an old scab.

Bill paid Dorset the money.

"How long can you hold him?" Bill asked.

"I'm not as strong as I used to be," Dorset told him.

"I can probably hold him for ten minutes."

"That's great!" Bill told him.

"I'll be halfway across the country by then."

Now I'm a fast runner.

But Bill took off even faster than me.

In fact, he was already a mile and a half outside of town

before I caught up with him.

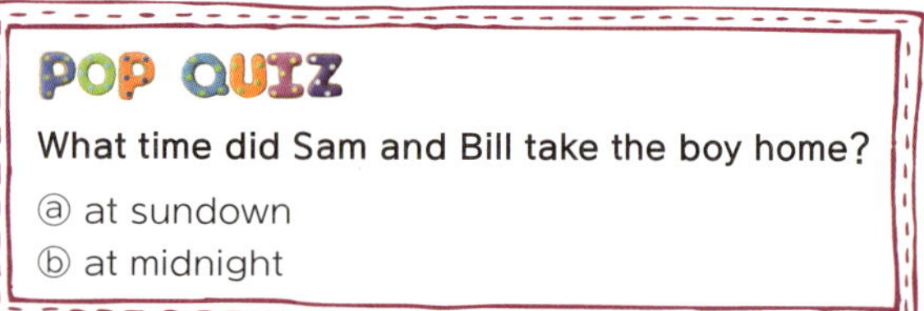

KEY WORDS

- knock
- peel off
- scab
- how long

- used to + *Verb*
- halfway
- across
- country

- runner
- in fact
- catch up with

Comprehension Quiz

A Choose the best answer to each question.

❶ Why did the Dorset boy seem like the best child to kidnap?

    a) He was the only son of a home loan banker.

    b) His mother loved him so much.

    c) The boy always followed the rules.

    d) He was very quiet and wouldn't cry.

❷ Why did the boy call himself Red Chief?

    a) Red Chief was his favorite character in a book.

    b) He was pretending to be an American Indian chief.

    c) He was wearing Red Chief shoes.

    d) Red Chief was the name of his favorite basketball team.

❸ Why didn't anyone care that the boy was kidnapped?

    a) No one noticed he was missing.

    b) The adults all thought he was in school.

    c) The schoolteacher thought he was at home sick.

    d) He was a troublemaker, and it was peaceful without him.

Across

❶ The boy called Sam Snake Eye the __________.

❸ Bill and Sam signed the note, "Two __________ Men."

❹ the last name of the boy's father

❻ money paid to get a person back from a kidnapper

Down

❷ The boy smashed a hot __________ on Bill's back.

❺ the name of the town

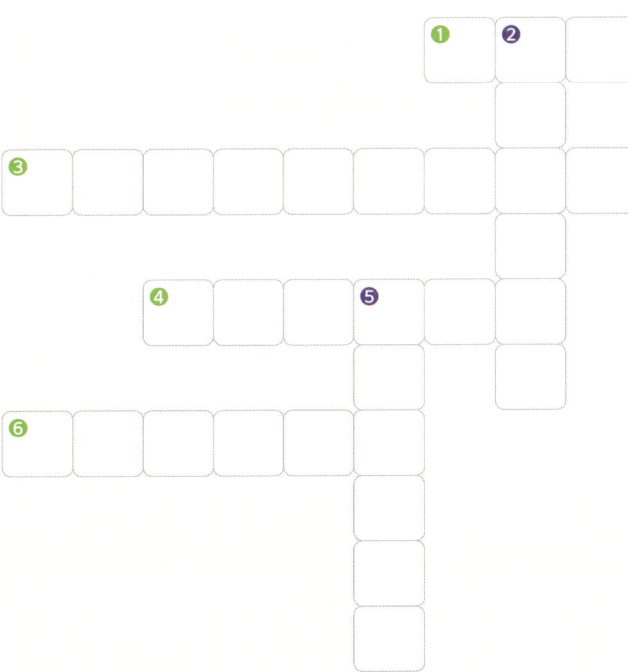

Let's Review the Story

Fill in the blanks to review the story.

Story 1

- **Title**: The Gift of the __________
- **Main Characters**: D__________ and J__________
- **Setting**: Della and Jim's a__________
- Della and Jim were too p__________. They didn't have money to buy gifts for each other. Della sold her __________. Jim sold his gold __________. They bought gifts for each other. They gave each other their g__________.

Story 2

- **Title**: The Witches' __________
- **Main Characters**: Miss M__________ and the G__________ man
- **Setting**: Miss Martha's b__________
- Miss Martha had a successful bakery, but she loved to daydream. She felt sorry for the G__________ man because she thought he was a poor a__________. She put b__________ in his loaves of bread and ruined his d__________. He called her an old w__________.

Story 3

- **Title**: The __________ of Red Chief
- **Main Characters**: B__________, S__________, and R__________ C__________
- **Setting**: S__________
- Bill and Sam k__________ a boy. They wanted $2,000 in r__________. The boy was so bad, they made the ransom $500 less. The boy's f__________ said the ransom was still too h__________. Bill paid the father $250 to take his boy back. The father held the boy while Bill and Sam r__________ out of town.

Let's Think & Talk

Think about the following questions and answer them freely.

❶ If you were Della and Jim, would you make the same choice as them? What present would you give your special person and how would you buy it?

❷ How would you feel if you harmed others unintentionally like Miss Martha? Have you ever hurt others with your own thoughts and behavior?

❸ If you were Sam and Bill, what would you do to the boy? Why?

Let's Review the Story

Story 1

- **Title**: The Gift of the **Magi**
- **Main Characters**: **Della** and **Jim**
- **Setting**: Della and Jim's **apartment**
- Della and Jim were too **poor**. They didn't have money to buy gifts for each other. Della sold her **hair**. Jim sold his gold **watch**. They bought gifts for each other. They gave each other their **gifts**.

Story 2

- **Title**: The Witches' **Loaves**
- **Main Characters**: Miss **Martha** and the **German** man
- **Setting**: Miss Martha's **bakery**
- Miss Martha had a successful bakery, but she loved to daydream. She felt sorry for the **German** man because she thought he was a poor **artist**. She put **butter** in his loaves of bread and ruined his **drawing**. He called her an old **witch**.

Story 3

- **Title**: The **Ransom** of Red Chief
- **Main Characters**: **Bill**, **Sam**, and **Red** **Chief**
- **Setting**: **Summit**
- Bill and Sam **kidnapped** a boy. They wanted $2,000 in **ransom**. The boy was so bad, they made the ransom $500 less. The boy's **father** said the ransom was still too **high**. Bill paid the father $250 to take his boy back. The father held the boy while Bill and Sam **ran** out of town.

After-reading Test

- O. Henry's Short Stories
- Level 3
- 27 Questions

(Vocabulary 7 / Reading Comprehension 16 /

Sentence Structure & Grammar 4)

1. Which of the following does NOT indicate a place?
   ① cave
   ② comb
   ③ salon
   ④ bakery

2. Which of the following does NOT indicate a person?
   ① feather
   ② farmer
   ③ customer
   ④ architect

3. Which of the following has the wrong past tense form of the verb?
   ① read – read
   ② hurt – hurt
   ③ hit – hit
   ④ bite – bite

※ Choose the right word for each blank. (4~5)

4.
> He was so proud ___________ that watch.

   ① in
   ② to
   ③ of
   ④ up

5.
> Maybe they were setting ____________ search parties to find the boy.

① at

② up

③ into

④ with

※ Choose the common word for the two blanks. (6~7)

6.
> • No one was hanging ____________ missing person signs.
> • The boy was sneaking ____________ behind him.

① against

② away

③ for

④ up

7.
> • We'll be done ____________ the job by midnight.
> • In fact, he was already a mile and a half outside of town before I caught up ____________ him.

① off

② with

③ away

④ into

※ Choose the right answer to each question about *The Gift of the Magi*. (8~12)

8. How does the story show that the characters are poor?

① They don't have any money in the bank.

② Della has just paid the rent on the apartment.

③ Things in the apartment are broken.

④ They are hungry and have no food.

9. Why did Della shed a tear when she decided to sell her hair?
① It was a tear of joy.
② Her hair was her most precious possession.
③ She had allergies.
④ She cut her finger on the scissors.

10. Why did Madame Sofronie want to buy Della's hair?
① No other customers would sell their hair.
② Della's hair was very long, thick and shiny.
③ She needed to make a wig for herself.
④ Della's hair smelled nice.

11. What did Jim use to carry his gold watch?
① a knotted string
② a fabric strap
③ an old leather band
④ an old metal chain

12. What did Jim do when Della told him to get out his watch?
① He fell on the couch and cried.
② He fell on the couch and smiled.
③ He told Della he would get it later.
④ He told Della he loved her.

※ Choose the right answer to each question about *The Witches' Loaves*. (13~17)

13. What did Miss Martha think about the German man after they talked about the painting?

    ① He must be lonely.
    ② He must be an art dealer.
    ③ He must have excellent eyesight.
    ④ He must be a genius.

14. Why did Miss Martha wear a pretty silk dress in her bakery?

    ① She hoped the German man would notice her.
    ② It was a celebration day.
    ③ She was taking a cake to a wedding party.
    ④ She always dressed up.

15. What did Miss Martha daydream about after the German man took the bread which she secretly had spread butter on?

    ① She daydreamed about where the man lived.
    ② She daydreamed that the man would be happy when he tasted the butter.
    ③ She daydreamed about how to spend her $2,000.
    ④ She daydreamed about new ideas for making a big cake.

16. What did the young man tell Miss Martha about the German man?

    ① He was a famous artist.
    ② He owned an art gallery.
    ③ He drew plans for architects.
    ④ He designed houses.

17. What did the young man tell Miss Martha is better than an eraser to erase pencil marks?

    ① a gum eraser

    ② a white eraser

    ③ stale bread

    ④ a tissue

※ Choose the right answer to each question about *The Ransom of Red Chief*. (18~23)

18. Why did Bill say the ransom was going to be $500 more?

    ① Bill found out the father had more money.

    ② Bill disagreed with his friend about how much money they needed.

    ③ The boy scratched Bill with his fingernails.

    ④ The boy hit Bill in the eye with a piece of a brick.

19. Where did Bill and Sam take the boy?

    ① They took him to a hotel in the next town.

    ② They took him to a cave in a nearby mountain.

    ③ They took him to a barn outside of town.

    ④ They hid him in an old copper mine.

20. What did Sam see when he woke up?

    ① Red Chief was sitting on Bill's chest and holding a knife.

    ② Bill was chained to a tree by a pirate.

    ③ Bill was tied to a stake to be burned.

    ④ Red Chief was whooping and dancing around the fire.

21. Why didn't Sam go back to sleep?

① He went back to sleep but had bad dreams.

② He had had too much coffee at dinner.

③ He remembered that Red Chief was going to burn him at the stake.

④ He wanted to take a walk in the moonlight.

22. What did Mr. Dorset tell Sam and Bill about the ransom? Choose two answers.

① "Your ransom is too high."

② "I will only pay you $250 for him."

③ "You pay me $250 and I'll take him back."

④ "I need some time to get the money."

23. What did Bill call the boy in the story? Choose two answers.

① a daredevil

② a wildcat

③ a monster

④ a brat

※ Choose the wrong part of each sentence. (24~25)

24.
She <u>wanted</u> to <u>buy Jim</u> <u>special</u> <u>something</u>.
　　① 　　② ③ 　　④

25.

26. What is the right answer in which both words correctly fit in each blank?

This town was ___________ flat ___________ a cast iron griddle.

① so, like
② so, as
③ as, as
④ as, so

27. What is the correct sentence?
① Here is how he works.
② Here are how he work.
③ Here is how does he work.
④ Here are how did he work.

Suzanne Pitner
Suzanne Pitner is a teacher and writer who has enjoyed visiting Alaska, exploring Rome, teaching in China, and is looking forward to more world travel. She has a Master's Degree in Education, and is a graduate of the Long Ridge Writer's Group. In addition to writing educational articles and books, she writes historical fiction and contemporary fiction for young adults using the pen name Suzanne Lilly.

O. Henry's Short Stories

Written by O. Henry
Retold by Suzanne Pitner
Illustrated by Taegyeom Cho

First Published in October 2017

Editorial Manager: Juyon Choi
Editors: Kyunghee Jang, Jiyeong Park
Designers: Eunhee Lee, Elim
Cover Designer: Eunhee Lee

Published and distributed by

Darakwon Bldg., 64-1 Jandari-ro, Mapo-gu, Seoul, Korea 04031
Tel: 82-2-736-2031(ext. 250)   Fax: 82-2-732-2037
Homepage: www.ihappyhouse.co.kr
Publisher: Kyudo Chung

ISBN: 978-89-6653-550-7 18740 / 978-89-6653-156-1 18740(set)

[Components]
• 1 Audio CD (Recording Studio: Aram)
• Answer Keys & Korean Translation: Free download at www.ihappyhouse.co.kr

Image Credit: shutterstock.com / Wikimedia Commons